Yes, I Can Taste

Yes, I Can

Book II

VELVIA D. NORMAN

ILLUSTRATED BY GEOVANNI LIVINGSTON,
LINETH CAROLINA HERNANDEZ

AuthorHouse™
1663 Liberty Drive
Bloomington, IN 47403
www.authorhouse.com
Phone: 833-262-8899

This book is printed on acid-free paper.

ISBN: 978-1-6655-2562-6 (sc)
ISBN: 978-1-6655-2563-3 (hc)
ISBN: 978-1-6655-2561-9 (e)

Library of Congress Control Number: 2021909808

Print information available on the last page.

Published by AuthorHouse 06/24/2021

authorHOUSE

Dedication

I am dedicating this second of the five-series Yes, I Can Collection to my six grandchildren: Hope, Heaven, Naisha, Bloom, Hezekiah and Harmony. I hope it inspires, encourages, and empowers them as they learn to read and identify items alphabetically.

A

Yes, I can taste an Apple.

B

Yes, I can taste a Banana.

Yes, I can taste a Cantaloupe.

D

Yes, I can taste Dates.

E

Yes, I can taste an Eggplant.

Yes, I can taste Figs.

Yes, I can taste Grapes.

H

Yes, I can taste Honeydew Melon.

I

Yes, I can taste Indian Figs.

Yes, I can taste a Jackfruit.

K

Yes, I can taste a kiwi.

L

Yes, I can taste a Lemon.

M

Yes, I can taste a Mango.

N

Yes, I can taste a Nectarine.

Yes, I can taste an Orange.

P

Yes, I can taste a Peach.

Yes, I can taste a Quince.

R

Yes, I can taste Raspberries.

Yes, I can taste Strawberries.

T

Yes, I can taste Tomatoes.

U

Yes, I can taste an Ugni.
(`ug-nee)

Yes, I can taste a Voavanga.
(`voh-ah-´van-gah)

W

Yes, I can taste a Watermelon.

X

Yes, I can taste a Xigua.
(`zi-gwah)

Y

Yes, I can taste a Yuza.
('yoo-zoo)

Z

Yes, I can taste a Zucchini.

Printed in the United States
by Baker & Taylor Publisher Services